TRUTH
EXPOSED

Fredy Denis

Copyright © 2016 by Fredy Denis

All rights reserved. No portion of this book may be reproduced, transmitted in any form or by any means-electronic, mechanical, photocopy, recording, or any other without the prior permission of the author.

Cover Design by Alonge Akinola A. (Pixondesignz)

ISBN-13: 978-1539041054

[Fredy Denis, Georgia, USA]

This book is dedicated to the abused and the abusers. I believe through prayer and confrontation there is hope for both.

St John 8: 1-11

The storylines presented in this book are not associated with the author. They are fictional, but yet real in the lives of many people. Brace yourself as the Truth is Exposed.

Contents

Preface	7
I Called Him Dad	9
Freedom	15
Incarceration	19
Just Sex ..Right	25
The Desire	31
Keep Praying	37
Strength	41
Addicted	45
Why	49
Taken	55
Make Dad Proud	61
The Funeral	65
My Baby	71
Procrastination	75
Deceived	79
Pimped	85
The Pen	91
Divided	95
The Confession	101
Life	109

Thoughts and desires bled on paper, expressing the heart

Jesus declared that we shall know the truth and the truth shall make us free (St. John 8:32). Imbedded within the lives of many are some uncovered truths, hidden deceit, deceptions, and a web of lies. These things have a way of squeezing the life out of an individual. It affects dreams, goals, families, churches, and nations. Through this book you'll find strength to confront these areas and take your life back. Secrets kill, but the truth reveals. What others are afraid to say, we expose.

I CALLED HIM DAD

From the store to the mall

Throwing the football in the yard

Dinners and movies

Family trips, playing video games, and playing cards

Lunches at school; he showed he cared

Though my real dad was gone, he was there

He embraced my hurt, sheltered my pain

At a young age he gave me a new song to sing

A new door of love, joy bells beginning to ring

After all the words spoken, someone finally believes in me

I called him DAD

Such an improvement came into my life

Grades elevated, attitude changed

Oh now I can see the light

Another family I have; new dreams I see

Once I doubted

But now something good will come out of me

Football practices, meetings at school

Parks, driving lessons, fishing adventures, and trips to the pool

Taught me to pray, taught me to read my bible

Taught me to dance with all my soul and fire

I called him DAD

Everything seemed so good, yes it seemed so right

Until the sun went down and the lights went out

Then it was night

The man that brought me joy, now brings me pain

What's happening, he's no longer the same

I lay in the bed grasping in fear

Eyes barely open as a shadow draws near

The covers are pulled back and he gets in bed

Soon following, I feel hands on my legs

I know these things shouldn't be

Who do I tell, who can help me

I love him like a father, but he's treating me like a mate

Daytime is great, but at night I see different traits

Now I'm confused and continually afraid

Yet I must confront this issue that has me shame

And I called him DAD

With my head held down

I say dad you're hurting me by what you do

He says son I know, I don't want to

Some nights would be good and I'd be glad

Because I knew if anyone ever knew

I'd lose the dad I never had

In church he preached, prayed, and laid hands

But after hours, those same hands were in my pants

I would close my eyes and attempt to play sleep

But uncertainty would grip me from the top of my body

Down to my feet

I didn't want to lose the one I called dad
But something must happen and happen fast

Things blew up as only time would reveal
Two people with broken hearts, one sent to jail

Liberty was granted and the healing could start
But for the rest of my life
He will be known as dad in my heart

And I called him DAD

FREEDOM

The battles that rage within my mind

As I'm faced with doing this time

I'm contemplating giving up

Closing shop, being quiet, and shutting up

I know my purpose, I've seen my goal

But my recent failures have pushed me in a dark hole

Who am I, what have I become

This is not a finished work; I know God is not done

I see the light but have no strength to reach

I've seen victory but yet trampled by defeat

I don't want to be the person I've been made

Made? Yes, because all of this did not come about in one day

How do I overcome, who can rescue me

Can life be restored to my feeble bones, oh Lord transform me

Do I want to be free or do I love being bound
Do I enjoy the pleasures of sin hanging around

My soul is at war, thoughts flooded with fears
My body weakened as my eyes shed tears

But I do believe that my deliverance will surely come
I'll get through this, I'll overcome

I refuse to die in this crucial state
With hands uplifted, I plead for God's grace

Grace to lift me up and to bring me through
Lord, bring my soul out of prison that it can praise you

INCARCERATED

Iron doors and brick walls

Isolated from society, stand by for chow call

Taking orders, following rules

No sunshine unless ordered by the crew in blue

Limited calls, variety denied

Be quiet, get up against the wall, or you won't go outside

Beating on your chest, rapping inside your head

Maintaining your sanity; I guess it's better than being dead

No privacy, don't speak of cushion; bed hard as bricks

Store call once a week, its free! No, I wish

Missing your family, remembering in your mind

Dreaming of freedom, disturbed by officer saying

Get up, its count time

Medicine calls, clipper shave, get by your bunk for inspection

Hands by your side, face forward, feet together

Throw him in the hole, teach him a lesson

Dorm orderly detail, buffing floors, moving bunks

Bush whacking, mowing grass

Dudes riding by with that beat in the trunk

Vegetable trays, squash, and macaroni

Red water; known as Kool-Aid, coffee cake, and bologna

Spades, dominoes, checkers, and casino

Basketball, NASCAR, football on TV

Some people playing uno

One style we all wear one motto we all follow

Lie down, chill out, and then look forward to tomorrow

Fights in the shower, arguing on the yard

Guards rush to the scene; too late, homeboy done fell hard

Church call, praises ringing, Friday evening bible study

Saturday and Sunday visitation; oh it's looking lovely

Sending out mail, standing by hoping to receive a letter

Special days, holidays approaching, it's got to get better

Big paper sack filled with goodies and all kinds off snacks
Switching, trading, wheeling and dealing
Boy my locker box is fat

One for two, maybe two for three
Got it till store day, but don't get silly and forget you owe me
Cigarette smoking, out of bugler; let's go fishing
Forbidden plants burning, piss test, somebody snitching

Dope boys lying, flossing and claiming to be some crooks
Had it all in the free world, can't get a dollar on the book
Alcohol anonymous, stand by for G.E.D class
I got mine on the street, but the record says you didn't pass

Clothing exchange, in the library one book at a time
Get naked, squat, grab, and cough; nothing you can hide

Measure your bed, tie your bag
Fold your clothes a certain way
Food in the back, cosmetics in the front
Do it right, the authorities don't play

Go see your counselor; what does she have to say

The answer is I don't know

You told me that the last time I came

Get in trouble, sign the paper, and receive a D-R

Go to court, extended stay, an added damper in the heart

Release papers, filled with cheer

Escape this life, departure is near

Jump in your bunk and cancel all your plans

Everything you do now concerns leaving the facility

And being a better person

Experience and learning

This side of the world has stop spinning

Name called, doors opened; here I go still winning

New joys ahead, nothing but sunshine I see

Past behind, future ahead, victory high

And defeat beneath

After all of this I made it

This is the life of a person who's been incarcerated

JUST SEX ....RIGHT

I turned on the water, preparing myself to take a shower

Giving my body a real good cleansing

For I knew I'd be leaving in an hour

You see I met someone this morning

And immediately we clicked

Made arrangements to experience each other's body

Yea; this is it

Hey, I can handle my own; I'm on my grown man tonight

I don't see anything wrong with a little bump and grind…right

Out of the shower into something quick

No need to get fancy, because once I spit that's it

No strings attached, no real connection, no emotional ties

No big deal; it's all good, it's just sex…. right

I've gathered my items, two condoms and a bottle of lube

Not much in the tube, but it's enough to make it slide through

Heading out the door I give her number a ring

She says meet me at hotel room number 119

I know that what's about to happen is not in God's plan

But can a brother have some slack, I'm only human

I enter the room and there she is, just like the picture said

I was slightly afraid to be cat fished

But I took the chance instead

Just sex ... right

While having sex the last condom I had broke

I pulled out, she pulls me in and says don't stop, let's go

Hey, she said she was clean, I don't think she'd lie

She looks too good to be sick, she's just too fine

Now I'm really feeling myself, I'm deep in the ocean

I'm losing my sense of paddle

Now I'm just stroking with the motion

This is one of the best nights I've had in my life

Sorry I can't cuff her, its jut sex ... right

I gather my clothes and grab my keys

The incident fresh in my mind

I head toward the door; she calls my name and says

Thanks for the ride

Three weeks later I was watching the news

While sitting on the couch

I see the girl I was with in handcuffs

So I proceeded to turn up the sound

The reporter states that she was arrested

For infecting people with aids

And that anyone who've had contact with her

Should get checked immediately

My heart dropped to the floor as my mouth was wide open

I really couldn't believe my ears

Is it true what was just spoken

I used two condoms but the second one broke

What a shame

That's why she didn't want me to stop

I thought it was my stroke game

What I'm supposed to do, how can I go on with life

This was not supposed to happen; it was just sex … right

THE DESIRE

I saw your profile, your picture; I viewed your page

I didn't want to be seen

So I didn't press like, I just silently walked away

I returned to look again

Pondering upon what my eyes could see

All of a sudden you liked one of my posts

That's when the desire began to stand up in me

I sent you a request

Following acceptance I said, thanks for the add

I send a smiley with a wink, because I really wanted to say

Can I get in your pants

You say no problem and leave it as that

Then the desire fades away, but oh, it'll be back

One night around midnight you post is there anybody up

I go to make my move

So I hit the inbox with … what's up

We begin to talk and I decide to share my life

What I've struggled with, how I want to change

From living wrong to living right

You begin to be transparent

Letting me know that you've struggled with the same thing

So now the desire stands up and begins to take wings

You go so far to tell me details of certain incidents

I listen while contemplating and say, oh; what a coincidence

The things you say, I've already known

Because I did my background work on you

Looking at every detail, hiding out and laying low

I even asked about you amongst some of our mutual friends

And your closest told me that you're about that life

And that you'd give in

Now that I got you right where I want you

I believe it's time that I make my move

I say I really needed this talk, can I get your number

You got Skype, Facetime, or Ovoo

You're so gullible that you believe I really want your help

You give me the digits, the details

And soon you'll give me something else

I leave the scene knowing that my story had an impact on you

And just like I thought

One day you hit me up saying, I'm just checking on you

Before you texted I posted a status saying

I'm down, I need a friend, and I need to talk

You being so caring and naive runs to the rescue

Not knowing you're about to fall

You say how can I help, I reply; can you Skype

You say give me a minute, I say ok in the text

But my mouth says tonight is the night

I press ignore the first time and I laugh when I see you call

You ask am I ok, I say call back

The desire in me says, not bad at all

I proceed to talk about some things that I'm going through

You do the normal and talk about Jesus and what he can do

I stand up from the camera to use the bathroom

Making sure you can see my shape

I quickly apologize and say

My bad, I tried to keep the camera on my face

Upon my return we chuckle and we laugh, I roll in the bed

I can tell you're feeling some type of way

Because you're no longer tensed you're relaxed instead

You feel more comfortable, so you open up a little more

The desire creeps upon me and then I open the door

I mention that I'm horny and that I need some help

You try to laugh it off and just smile

Turn your head and look somewhere else

You see I've heard about you, and I know what you do
Matter of fact, to be exact
The person you shared those nude pictures with last year
Sent them to me too

You claim to be delivered but tonight I will put it to the test
Will you back down, or will you give in like the rest

Your post says I love God, your pictures say I'm churchy
Now that I got you to myself, I want to see if you can work it

All of a sudden you get a call and say that you have to go
You may have gotten away tonight
But this desire will show up again
Whether it's in me or someone else you know

KEEP PRAYING

Church was on point, the Spirit was high

The word that was given spoke volumes into my life

The praise was definitely there, the praise team took me in

I felt like something great was happening

Something great happening within

I fell on the floor, to my surprise I began to roll

From the left to the right

Something was taking place in my soul

I got up all drunk, like I'd drunk some vodka

Some people looking at me

Like what happened was a big shocker

I left the service on cloud nine

Believing that nothing could bring me down

Skip to the loo my darling, oh what joy I've found

I stepped outside the church and got on the church van

All of a sudden I hear no more music

And reality begins to sink in

The songs the choir sung have faded from my ear

That high fiving neighbor is nowhere near

They approach my house and I get off the van

I put the key in the door and think to myself, I am home alone ….again

No dancing partner to grab me by the hand

No one for me to shout at or say amen

I'm rushed with feelings of grief, loneliness, and regret

After all that dancing I did

How can my emotions be in this big of a wreck

I'm bombarded with the things that aren't yet solved

The prayers not yet answered, the situations not yet resolved

My faith tells me just to believe

But as I look around the present is all I see

I go to the kitchen

To fix a plate of the food I made the night before

Sit down to eat, only me, yep once again, yes once more

I just came from church, where is the high that I felt

Was it for real, why has it all left

I thought all I needed was my praise

But now something is telling me that was just a phase

I lay down to relieve my heart of the pressure that I feel

I say God I know where I am, but I also know you're real

The pain intensifies and so does the tears

I'm fighting to be strong, but I don't know if I will

I'm silently listening to see what God may be saying

From my inner most being I hear, just keep praying

STRENGTH

As you close your eyes, preparing to get some rest

Tears fill your eyelids because there's a lot on your chest

You drift off to sleep, to your pillow you cling

And all of a sudden you hear a ding

Your inbox lights up, you have a message from a friend

Your desire is to ignore it

But the other part of you longs to see what's within

You open it to see a smiley face, a wink, a heart, and a kiss

All of a sudden sleep is no longer necessary

And now you're caught up in pure bliss

You've waited so long just to get their attention

Emotions are high, adrenalin is pumping

Your eyes are even twitching

You know if you respond you may fall into sin

But a piece of you says, let sin win

What shall you do, it's like a dream come true
The one you've always been interested in
Is now interested in you

You type your response but you don't press send
The strength within you says this has to end

You pull yourself together, and you press delete
Giving strength to victory and casting down defeat

You turn over, grabbing your pillow and your bible
Which is in arm's length
Gripping it you say Lord, thank you for strength

ADDICTED

I'm running, running, trying to get away

I'm fighting the same battle every single day

How do I win the fight over something that's attached to me

Emotions, desires, pulling at me

It's one thing to be addicted and ask for help

But what do you do when you're addictive to yourself

No matter where I go I'm faced with this one thing

That what's going on is within me

My eyes visualize and my heart yearns

My spirit rejects, but the passion burns

I know my feelings are only a deception

But maybe the deception is in my perception

Am I dealing with something that may be true

How can that be

When the bible declares that this is something not to do

I flee to my bed so that I can escape thru sleep

But my night is full of the lust thereof

Attacking me in my dreams

It awakes me and causes me to shake like a feen needing a fix

Sending my body into rages like a heroin attic needing a hit

So full of death, selfishness, and pride

I stand-I stand

But I'm not sure how long I'll stay alive

I want someone to blame, who will pay the penalty

No one, because this issue is not with others

This issue is with me

Who can see my vulnerability and come to my need

Don't get too close, you don't want to catch this disease

A plague, oh it's just like leprosy

The only thing, it's imbedded internally

Looking from the outside, everything is just fine

But if you could see what's in my head

You'd be shocked to know what's on my mind

Don't know how long this will go on

For how many days or years

How many nights, how many seasons, how many tears

Though it's hard, I mustn't break

Being addicted to masturbation

Is one of the worst things someone could face

WHY

Drugs, violence, murder, deceit

Jealousy over territory, demise and defeat

My block, your block, representing the hood

Bullets flying, blades swinging, everything misunderstood

½ pound of mid, a pound of pert

Line of coke, baby I got the works

Hennessey, crown royal, old english, grey goose

Lights out, DJ spinning, club popping, everybody getting loose

West side, east side, blood, and crypts

Smoke in the air, drink in my cup

Too good to gulp, just sip

Dope boys tricking, young girls slipping

Married and single, late night tipping

Frauds and schemes

Cross you out for 2 tens, 6 ones, and two twenties

Take you down, swipe your card

Got any work; what you want soft or hard

Up your nose, in your vein

Feel the fire, experience the pain

Gangs and thugs sparing no life

Kids, authorities, mama, nor wife

Big boy rides and big boy whips

Give me your check on the 1st and on the third it will flip

But Why

What does it profit, what does it give

To live this life but not to live

Temporary satisfaction, never at ease

Slipping and sliding, deceptive peace

Gathering and storing, putting it away

But when the funk hits the fan, everyone has to pay

Dodging the lights, don't be no snitch

Jack boys coming, feen want a fix

Doors kicked in, stacks uncovered

Hands up, get on the ground, now cuff them

Time given that cannot be returned

Forever being taught but failing to learn

Cycle of confusion, confinement never ending

Make a few dollars, double that in spending

But Why

As valuable as life is, why waste it on what brings no value

Vapors of air, smoke screen, crashes, shattering

Casting your pearls only before the swine

False hope, false dreams, from dollars to dimes

Spending days chasing a chase that cannot be grasped

Envying and conspiring to get what another haves

Murder my cat, I murder your dog

Pluck my chicken, I slice your hog

Take from the house, give it to the streets

Sell it for the low

$5, $10, all I want is a blow

So high, so high, so high, now I'm high

So low, so low, so low, now I'm low

Reality settles in and shuts down the show

Months, days, and years all gone

Age done caught up, yet no place to call home

Now at the end, everything meaningless and nothing right

You're eating the path you've chosen for your life

But Why

TAKEN

I remember like it was yesterday; it's all coming in so clear
My fingers gripped to the bed, my heart pounding in fear

You see I thought it was just an outing
And we were only friends
Never did I know my innocence would be taken

It started out so cool, just me and my boy
Acting silly, hanging out, making a lot of noise

We went to the mall to get some shoes
Then later we went to the bar
We even talked to a few females
Who said they were going to the park

A few drinks, nothing strong
But that one bathroom visit
Must've been the biggest mistake of all

Now I'm feeling woozy and dizzy; things are a little blurry
The ground is rocking, I'm standing still
People around moving in a hurry

I remember being in his car, headed down the road

I'm fighting to stay conscious

But whatever he put in my drink is taking control

Next, I wake up in a bed unfamiliar to me

Hands unzipping my pants, feeling strange to me

My clothes ripped off

Why is this dude kissing me on my cheek

I'm really trying to get up, but my body is too weak

I utter the words No, but they seemingly go unheard

That's when I'm flipped over, my faced shoved in a pillow

So I can say no more words

I'm penetrated, oh the pain I feel

How could my homie do me like this

Is this a dream or is this real

I thought he liked girls, we've hollered at the same chicks

I'm so wounded, how can I ever forget this

What must I do, my whole life has been took

My pride and my self-esteem has just been shook

It's all playing back to a day we were on 4th Ave

When he made the comment

Boy, you got the biggest butt a man could have

How could I be so naïve, how'd I not see

My homie don't like girls, he likes ME!

If I kill him, I'll end up doing 25 to life

If I tell anyone, they'll think I'm gay…..right

Tossed between the two

Questions rattling my brain

OMG! What if I got an STD, this punk has got to pay

Did I lead this on, I thought we were cool

Yea, I may have said a few homo jokes a time or two

Only if I were bigger, maybe he wouldn't have tried me

Being skinny and scrubby; this dude had already sized me

Pillow flooded with tears, I feel so forsaken

My world is crushed; my manhood has just been taken

MAKE DAD PROUD

I have goals; I have a mission to achieve

To make my dad proud is one of my biggest dreams

I know he'll be happy, if he could see me now

I can visualize the look on his face

Mouth dropped, saying WOW

I'm just what he said I'd be

I'm a product of his mentality

He looked me in the face

And uttered these powerful words one day

He said son when you grow up

You're going to be gay

At that moment I immediately burst in tears

Not knowing the impact it would have on me

Throughout the years

I was fine in my adolescence

The teenage years I made it through

But around 20 and 21, other desires begin to form

Other things I begin to do

Its ok, no need for me to be down

Because I'm finally starting to live out my dream

Of making my daddy proud

Too bad he can't see me in action, see me work my magic

From man to man, bed to bed

I was letting them have it

No fear, why be afraid

As long as daddy is proud, everything will be ok

But dad didn't tell me about the heartbreaks

Visits to the clinics, possible outbreaks

You see, living out this dream has cost me valuable time in life

My ability to naturally produce kids; possibility of having a wife

Pouring my seed into ground that can't produce

False pleasures, temporary satisfaction, but no fruit

Now on my death bed I'm dying of aids

Soon they'll put me in the ground

But as least I can say I fulfilled my dream

Of making my daddy proud

THE FUNERAL
FROM A DAUGHTER

Sitting in this funeral, trying to come to some point of relief
Overwhelmed in tears and swallowed by grief

The woman that carried me in her body and took care of me
The one who breast fed me during the stages of my infancy

She lies in this casket, lifeless with her hands on her chest
Voices filling the air with songs, as people show their respects

Sitting by my grandmother on the front row
We are known as the bereaves
All of us are in tears
But they don't know the real reason why I grieve

My mother and I recently got into an argument
She was giving me some advice but I got on the defense

I felt like I knew what was best for me
Why she got to be in my business, I'm 17 you see

I could handle my own business, I know about life
I didn't need her governing my affairs….right

I stormed out the house and I slammed the door

But before I left, I told her to hell she could go

She made me mad, treating me like a child

So I went to move in with my 32 year old boyfriend for a while

I never went back to see mom, or even called

And now I'm in this funeral

Never got the chance to apologize to her at all

The time came for people to give remarks

So I stand up and toward the microphone I begin to walk

With my head down

I take the microphone and walk towards the casket

The crowd looks astonished

Not knowing what's about to happen

I look at my mom's body and I begin to say

Mom, I'm sorry for what happened the other day

You were right and I was wrong

I should've never let my pride keep me away this long

I know you can't hear me but I wish you could

Things were never supposed to be this way

If you'd come back, I promise I'll act like I should

I need you to help me finish high school

Who'll see me off to my prom

Where will I go for advice

Get up, I need you mom

At this moment I'm hugged by my grandmother

And taken to my seat

She whispers in my ear and says, it's ok

Your mother is at peace

The words sound good, but I know the truth

My mother died from a broken heart

And now mine is broken too

While with her, she'd not yet received Christ in her life

So my belief is when I told her to go to hell

The following week she took flight

MY BABY

The moment has finally arrived that I've been waiting for
The birth of my first child, the delivery knocking at the door

I prayed for a son, and a son is what he gave
Come on baby Jr, I'm ready to see you today

As I hold my girl's hand
She begins to push with all her might
I say breathe
She says, you know I'm gone get you right

I'm so excited that the words don't even faze me
My joy is set before me, today I'm a daddy

He's brought home and the life begins
Raising, nurturing, facing challenges

I do my best to be the best role model I can be
Doing everything that my dad never done for me

From the cradle to his first class at head start

From playing in the sand, to the walks in the park

Everything was going good, just like I wanted it to be

Until I was hit with child support papers

At the start of the week

You see me and my girl have been together for 12 years

But our relationship had been rocky

And we concluded that it was best just to stop it

I always vowed to take care of my child

I assured her she didn't have to worry

I'd be there all the while

Now my son is ten and she says she needs some extra income

I told her to get a job and then she'll have a better outcome

When it comes to my son, I'm always about doing what's right

So I decide to just go with the flow and not put up a fight

We get in court and the judge calls our name

He says I have some interesting findings

Mam, is this the guy whom you're trying to get to pay

She says yes your honor, is there a problem

He says yes, according to the blood test

This guy here is not the father

Immediately my emotions shoot to the roof

I was in so much rage the bailiff had to pull me out

Because they feared what I'd do

Ten years of life devoted to a lie

This is the type of stuff that makes grown men cry

She sees me in the hallway but couldn't look me in the face

Shattered by deception

The results proving, that's not my baby

PROCRASTINATION

Wake up, turn over, and hit the snooze on the clock
I got work to do, but a few more minutes won't hurt

I should be up handling business, making major moves
But this bed feels so good, what am I supposed to do

I'm going to be a star, I see myself going many places
My name will ring in the ears of many; I'll be on big stages

I'll go to college and I'll maintain a 4.0 GPA
Mom will be very proud of me one day

I'll get my bachelor's degree and move on to my masters
Any woman will be eager to have me

I'll open my own business, hire my own people
Go to a church with a big white steeple

I'll live in a nice house; have a wife and three kids
Have a substantial amount of money in my accounts
Own a Mercedes and a Benz

I'll give back to my community

Host events and spread the love

Mentor a child and give them something they can be proud of

I'll run for a governmental office, and I'll win

I'll make changes in my city

I'll be the candidate that the people can believe in

All of these dreams I desire to fulfill

But only if I can fight against my own will

My will to lie in this bed just a few more seconds

They turn into minutes, into hours

I'll get up soon, I reckon

Days turn into months, and months into years

Where I once believed, now has been turned into fears

Age has caught me and my strength is starting to fail

I've lived my life, but never lived

I talked a good game, I gave a good speech

The words I'd speak would make anyone believe

I've waited too long, my actions were few

Now I'm stuck in the same place I started

Still saying what I'm going to do

I had the vision, I had the plan

My only problem was that

Procrastination was my best friend

DECEIVED
A DEVIL'S PERSPECTIVE

You've been told that I'm the father of lies

And that I've been that way from the beginning

Well, that's true, but I'm still winning

I'm winning because you know all my tricks and my devices

But yet you still let me live inside you

You quote the scriptures with such authority

But when it comes down to me or God

In your life I'm the majority

You say you love God, I believe you just love his benefits

Because you spend more time with me getting your needs met

I love it when you play that music; oh you do it so well

Those runs you do with your lips give me the chills

But it's not enough power in that

To cause you to leave me alone

You brought me to church, and now you're taking me home

You're on fire from the praise break

But as soon as that calms down I'll be in your ear

Because I got something g to say

You see I don't make your choices, I'm just the persuader

You open the door for me, and I become the invader

You believe the lie that just a little bit doesn't hurt

Then you're consumed by it, you're my slave, for me you work

I love the way you moan in your prayers

You get the crowd going by squalling when you preach

But I'll be waiting on you in your office

To watch you pull out your glass and take that drink

Oh, just a sip, oh just a gulp, oh just a bottle

Now you're an addicted preacher

Feening for your next swallow

I get excited while you're in church
Shouting that you're a winner
You see I don't mind you doing that
Because your kids are at home
Getting molested by the babysitter

But don't worry; it's all about you getting your blessing
Seeking for a better day on your way to heaven

While your children are building their resume
To become a thug, drug dealer, maybe even a prostitute
Your chasing recognition from the pastor
Leaving your kids to do what they want to do

But there is one thing that I can't stand
A believer who sincerely obeys God's commands

I like to prey on those who're not fully persuaded
Those who're churchy
But believe in having a wife and an old lady

I pervert the gospel by using one of their own
Hey, they'll listen to him
He has a congregation size that can fit in a dome

I love to prey on those who don't read the word
Because they can be easily misled
I can twist the scriptures to mean what I want
Use it to seduce them right in my bed

They really got power over me
But they can't make up their mind
They embrace God with one hand
While scratching my back on the other side

Double mined people, like the waves of the sea
Not knowing they've been deceived
Until they've been deceived

PIMPED

Mic check, mic check, somebody turn me up

You know what time it is, you already know what's up

It's offering time; some call it seed time and harvest

Bring out the biggest buckets, we're about to have a party

I must be strategic about this, don't want to scare you away

You can't know that you're being pimped on the Lord's Day

There are many strategies that I can use to reel you in

Since you love to dance

I guess with the praise music we'll begin

I'll crank that praise up so high, and make you feel so free

Tell you that the spirit is moving

And that you should be at liberty

Liberty to give, come on now let's dig deep

Make you feel guilty by saying Jesus paid the ultimate price

So don't be cheap

I could say I'll start this offering off with one hundred dollars
And then get four of my people to follow

That way it'll encourage others to get in line
Not knowing when we get in the back
Me and my crew is getting our money back; every dime

I could use my guessing skills and my gift of gab to lure you in
You're a prophecy junkie this one will be my big win

I'll call a couple people out
And prophesy a couple houses and cars
Maybe give them a check in the mail
A husband, a wife, or a new job

Who doesn't want more, greed is the center of it all
Then the rest will follow hoping their name I'll call

How about I tell them that they'll get it in seven days
By the time the seventh day comes
I'll be racking in money in another state

I'm on a roll, I'm living the life

Hey, if I don't get it somebody is getting it.... right

I got cars, homes, I got bling

For every finger on my hand I got a ring

A church full of chumps, a crowd full of wimps

Not even knowing they're being pimped by the pimp

Everything is lovely, everything is right

Until a stroke creeps upon my body one night

I'm lying in the hospital bed, in a coma and cannot move

My spirit begins to leave my body

Then I hear a voice laughing at me saying, you fool

I'm carried to a hallway which is completely dark

The heat that's expelled from the walls

Begin to put fear in my heart

The voice says you thought you were smart

You thought you were the man

But you were only being used as my agent

Welcome to your new home, well laid with fire

None of your riches gained by deception can help you now

You were deceiving while being deceived

And for the rest of eternity you'll be eternally grieved

You believed you were so cool, walking with that limp

You thought you were pimping

But you were just being pimped

THE PEN

It was a pen that gave me my very first grade

Sitting in elementary class

I remember it like it was yesterday

Wow time goes by so fast

It was a pen that my hand guided to do my homework

100 divided by 5 is 20

Had to prove how I got it, no short cuts

It was a pen that wrote me out my first check

Boss man says I got to pay you under the table

You're not old enough to have a legal job yet

It was a pen that gave me my first reprimand

Tried to explain it, but my mother didn't understand

She said put the pen and paper aside and hold out your hand

It was a pen that signed off on my first car

Not knowing that same pen would decide after non-payment

To repossess it out my yard

It was a pen that agreed to my first rental lease

Had to pay $175 a month

Looking back on it now, I can say that was very cheap

It was a pen that passed down the judgment from the judge

Sentencing me to jail time

Bars, confinement, incarceration

But not for a long time

After looking at the power of a pen

I begin to re-write my life

Correcting some faulty decisions

Bringing myself into alignment with what's right

I take the pen and I declare that I'll be the best I can be

My head shall not be lowered but raised above my enemies

I write that I'll succeed in all my endeavors and dreams

Procrastination and laziness shall not be a part of me

I shall have more than enough to meet my needs

Furnish my wants and help those achieve that I lead

The pen has been used to set up my demise

But I take the pen and use it to create a story

In line with God's will for my life

I take the pen and I cancel out all the writings against me

Negative words and accusations pinned to me

The rest of my story shall be filled with excitement and vigor

For I know that I win

The pen that wrote my beginning, now writes my end

DIVIDED

Shots ringing, shots fired

Two men standing up, one on the ground

Cameras rolling, people gripping their hearts in fear

Man down, man down, move; let the paramedics over here

The nation in an uproar, cities divided

White cop shoots black teenager, reason undecided

Was color a factor, or were they just doing their job

Is this the perfect time to pull out the race card

A mother loses a son, officer gains paid vacation

Security, protection, and moved to another station

Riots, looting, protesting in the streets

Everybody claiming to be an activist

But some need to have several seats

Families discombobulated, they want answers
Waiting on the video to be released
Knowing it has probably been tampered

Cellphone evidence uploaded to social media
People rushing to judgment
Some saying I don't believe it

Race war inciting, the truth being revealed
Friends that were pro black
Are now saying that nigger should've been killed

The details surface concerning the incident
The conclusion is, he was an unarmed teen
Headed to a church event

His clothing was dark
And he resembled a suspect in a homicide case
So they proceeded with caution
While meeting the young man face to face

His hands were in his pocket

While walking he was listening to his favorite beat

Surrounded by cops now yelling hands in the air

He's startled by what he sees

As he pulls his hands out of his pocket

His phone hits the ground

Thinking it was a gun, the cops let out a couple of rounds

Identity mistaken, was it his clothing, was it his hat

Or was it the tone of his skin called black

Profiled, picked out, and murdered like a beast

No respect given to his body, hours lying in the street

They killed purpose, they killed a dream

A young man graduating high school

Headed to Morehouse University

Tensions are high, while the world awaits the decision

Will the cops be charged, or will they get away with it

Security everywhere, knowing it can go both ways

If the cops are found not guilty

The streets will once again be filled with rage

The verdict is in; the DA has rendered a solution

The cops will not be charged but will receive further training

That's our conclusion

The country still divided, we need a new plan

For a nation divided against itself

Will not stand

CONFESSION
THE LETTER

From: Mr. Neal

To: Mr. Just Real

I recall being on your prayer line one morning
And you were speaking on confrontation
I was so overwhelmed with conviction
That writing you became an obligation

You encouraged us to be free
And to release those things that had us in a mental prison
So here am I
It's a lot; I hope you got time to listen

I guess I'll start from when I was a child
Running around with a runny nose
Putting everything in my mouth

I believe I was three years old
My mother wanted to go to the club
So she had my cousin to come over and babysit us

It was me and my brother who was ten

And my cousin who watched us was fifteen

Sitting on the couch

Looking at movies on the TV

My cousin would go to the room

And in a few minutes he would call my brother

The door would close, and then it would be minutes

Before we saw each other

I wasn't sure what they were doing, because I was too young

But my brother always came out crying

I said to myself, whatever it is, it can't be fun

It wasn't till later that I found out what was taking place

My cousin was taking his private part

And putting it on my brothers face

My brother told our mother

But they decided to keep it in the family

No cops were called and everybody seemed cool

Until, unto me it started happening

As I look back I blame my mother

Because she could've prevented it

But because she loved to party

She continued to let him babysit

One day when I was 12, I found my birth certificate

To my surprise the man I called daddy name was not on it

I asked around until I got the truth, which was very sad

I'm the product of a rape

My dad is my granddaddy and my granddaddy is my dad

I started getting into trouble

Stealing, vandalizing, and fighting

I knew no other way to express myself

I had a lot of rage inside of me

I started hanging with the thugs

They were chasing the girls who were fine and cute

This led to my first sexual experience

In the back of a car with a prostitute

At the age of 17

I ended up going to juvenile doing time for burglary

That's when I came into contact with a dude named Chris

Who introduced me to homosexuality

When I got out, I hid my desires

Tried to focus on being better in life

I was 18; I figured it was time I started to do what was right

I joined this church in the community

Where all the youth went

They had fun nights and concerts

They always had youth events

I befriended a dude that was the assistant on the youth team

He was close to my age, he was twenty

He was very compassionate and full of love

A lot that I didn't know he taught me

He called me his little bro

Everything was going good; things seemed to be falling in place

Until I needed to make a call

And had to use his phone one day

I had to be careful with it, because the phone was cracked

I ended my call

Then an app popped up on the screen called jackd

I was so curious, so I downloaded it when I got home

Put in my information

From that moment my life begin to take a turn of it's on

You see this was a sex app

That allowed you to meet people within close range

I didn't put my picture up, and I also used a fake name

I was so shocked to see how the app worked

I would turn it on even when I was in church

I just knew there wouldn't be many people on it in there

But I met most of my partners

Sitting three rows back in another chair

I wasn't open with it; I tried to keep it on the low

I knew I wanted to be a preacher so I couldn't let it all show

I figured I would get married to cover up the desires that I had

Maybe if I get a wife things will be better

I heard your story, I know you understand

So I found this girl who is so beautiful

We date and then we marry

I've told her many things, but I never told her of my sexuality

It's been two years and life is just what it is

I'm still holding on to my secret

Keeping people out of my business

That's where you come in

I'm listening to you preach on the line

And I'm overwhelmed by my sins

It's like I was standing in the mirror

Being confronted from within

I didn't know who to tell, I really don't know what to do

So I'm making the steps to correcting my life

Starting off by writing this confession to you

So uncertain and limited are our days

Numbered by someone higher

Who can understand His ways

Gathered amongst the grains formed in his hand

Predestined from the foundation of the universe

To carry out his plan

It's not always easy, but it's always worth it

We live then we die, but is that our only purpose

Are we here to suffer, shall we only experience pain

You may say no, but I'm fixed on the girl born with cancer

I believe Keisha is her name

Or the boy born with a disability

Confined to a wheelchair with limited mobility

The woman who's never been able to have kids

Because she was raped at a young age by several men

Who's at fault, is she to blame

So the question is why she must forever carry the shame

Life is like a riddle that can never be solved

Sometimes we just have to go with the flow and trust in God

As you've read the previous chapters

You ran across some words that brought you joy

Some that brought you laughter

But some were a reminder of the things you've hidden

Tucked away in a secret place

Things that make you cringe, that put a mirror to your face

You may have been perpetrated,

Or you may have been the perpetrator

But what stands true, is that both are in need of the Savior

Deep within our closets are skeletons that we deny

Covered up with smiles and grins

A concept called living a lie

Honestly, some of those skeletons aren't yet dead
They're breathing, functioning, and living inside our head

We dress them up with religion, labor, and good deeds
Covered up by deception while our soul continues to bleed

Never embracing the truth, continuing in falsehood
The outside looks nice, but the inside is no good

Know that there is hope for you
Whichever side of the spectrum you've found yourself in
The fact that you're breathing
Means you haven't reached your end

Confront the areas in your life that need healing
Bring those deeds to the light, confess it, and reveal it

With prayer and grace you'll be just fine
Because God has a way of restoring lost time

Seek forgiveness from those you've hurt

Forgive those who've hurt you

Get yourself together

Bring your thoughts into alignment with the truth

If counseling is deemed necessary, make it a priority

Make amends, give restitution, it's your life, take authority

No matter who's wrong, no matter who's right

We must understand everybody has a chapter in their book

And that chapter is called life

Contact Information

justrealbooks@gmail.com

Made in the USA
Monee, IL
12 May 2021